Gifts of Nature

BEGINNINGS

National Wildlife Federation

BEGINNINGS

5 Song to Pull Down the Clouds .... *Papago Indian Poem*

6 A Sense of Wonder .... *Rachel Carson*

8 Return of the Geese .... *Aldo Leopold*

10 Mountain Birth .... *Douglas Chadwick*

14 Fueled .... *Marcie Hans*

16 Good Morning, America .... *Carl Sandburg*

18 Peeping in the Shell .... *Faith McNulty*

24 Serendipity in the Bronx .... *E.B. White*

26 When Spring Came .... *Tlingit Indian Song*

30 Everyday Miracles .... *Annie Dillard*

32 Mushrooms .... *Sylvia Plath*

34 Frogs, Frogs, Frogs .... *Sue Hubbell*

36 The Greening of Summer .... *Ann Zwinger*

40 Rebirth of a Mountain .... *Ed Barnes, Donna Haupt, George Howe Colt*

42 Autumn Renewal .... *Henry David Thoreau*

44 March 9 .... *Hal Borland*

46 Credits

SONG TO PULL DOWN THE CLOUDS

At the edge of the world
It is growing light.
Up rears the light.
Just yonder the day dawns,
Spreading over the night.

Papago Indian song

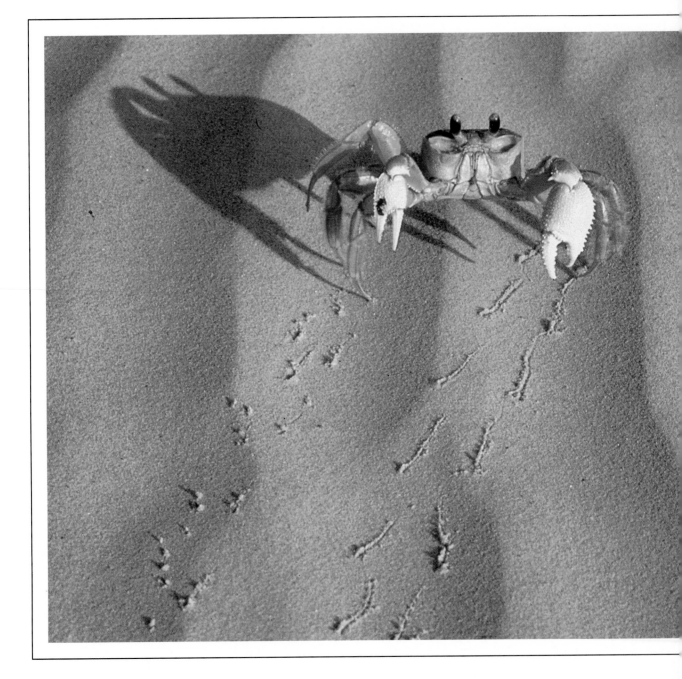

A SENSE OF WONDER

One stormy autumn night when my nephew Roger was about twenty months old I wrapped him in a blanket and carried him down to the beach in the rainy darkness. Out there, just at the edge of where-we-couldn't-see, big waves were thundering in, dimly seen white shapes that boomed and shouted and threw great handfuls of froth at us. . . .

A night or two later the storm had blown itself out and I took Roger again to the beach, this time to carry him along the water's edge, piercing the darkness with the yellow cone of our flashlight. . . .

Our adventure on this particular night had to do with life, for we were searching for ghost crabs, those sand-colored, fleet-legged beings which Roger had sometimes glimpsed briefly on the beaches in daytime. But the crabs are chiefly nocturnal, and when not roaming the night beaches they dig little pits near the surf line where they hide, seemingly watching and waiting for what the sea may bring them. For me the sight of these small living creatures, solitary and fragile against the brute force of the sea, had moving philosophic overtones, and I do not pretend that Roger and I reacted with similar emotions. But it was good to see his infant acceptance of a world of elemental things, fearing neither the song of the wind nor the darkness nor the roaring surf, entering with baby excitement into the search for a "ghos."

It was hardly a conventional way to entertain one so young, I suppose, but now, with Roger a little past his fourth birthday, we are continuing that sharing of adventures in the world of nature that we began in his babyhood, and I think the results are good. The sharing includes nature in storm as well as calm, by night as well as day, and is based on having fun together rather than on teaching.

* * *

A child's world is fresh and new and beautiful, full of wonder and excitement. It is our misfortune that for most of us that clear-eyed vision, that true instinct for what is beautiful and awe-inspiring, is dimmed and even lost before we reach adulthood. If I had influence with the good fairy who is supposed to preside over the christening of all children I should ask that her gift to each child in the world be a sense of wonder so indestructible that it would last throughout life, as an unfailing antidote against the boredom and disenchantments of later years, the sterile preoccupation with things that are artificial, the alienation from the sources of our strength.

Rachel Carson

RETURN OF THE GEESE

One swallow does not make a summer, but one skein of geese, cleaving the murk of a March thaw, is the spring. A cardinal, whistling spring to a thaw but later finding himself mistaken, can retrieve his error by resuming his winter silence. A chipmunk, emerging for a sunbath but finding a blizzard, has only to go back to bed. But a migrating goose, staking two hundred miles of black night on the chance of finding a hole in the lake, has no easy chance for retreat. His arrival carries the conviction of a prophet who has burned his bridges.

A March morning is only as drab as he who walks in it without a glance skyward, ear cocked for geese.

I once knew an educated lady, banded by Phi Beta Kappa, who told me that she had never heard or seen the geese that twice a year proclaim the revolving seasons to her well-insulated roof. Is education possibly a process of trading awareness for things of lesser worth? The goose who trades his is soon a pile of feathers.

The geese that proclaim the seasons to our farm are aware of many things, including the Wisconsin statutes.

The south-bound November flocks pass over us high and haughty, with scarcely a honk of recognition for their favorite sandbars and sloughs. "As a crow flies" is crooked compared with their undeviating aim at the nearest big lake twenty miles to the south, where they loaf by day on broad waters and filch corn by night from the freshly cut stubbles. November geese are aware that every marsh and pond bristles from dawn till dark with hopeful guns.

March geese are a different story. Although they have been shot at most of the winter, as attested by their buckshot-battered pinions, they know that the spring truce is now in effect.

They wind the oxbows of the river, cutting low over the now gunless points and islands, and gabbling to each sandbar as to a long-lost friend. They weave low over the marshes and meadows, greeting each newly melted puddle and pool.

Finally, after a few *pro-forma* circlings of our marsh, they set wing and glide silently to the pond, black landing-gear lowered and rumps white against the far hill. Once touching water, our newly arrived guests set up a honking and splashing that shakes the last thought of winter out of the brittle cattails. Our geese are home again!

Aldo Leopold

MOUNTAIN BIRTH

The nanny on the northernmost cliff had gradually stopped keeping company with the rest of the herd in the upper valley. For the past several days her movements had been confined to ledges about halfway down the outcropping of tile-red argillite rock. It was one of the cliff's steepest sections. Several of the ledges, though, were overhung by stone shelves that offered some shelter in case the weather turned foul. These were the ones she frequented.

The last week of May had just arrived. Across the terraced rock and lower meadows the last flattened brown husks of long-frozen vegetation were quickly disappearing beneath a swelling green. Meltwater poured over cliff faces everywhere in glistening waterfalls as deep snowpacks toward the summit softened. Farther down the valley the new needles of western larch shone like green fire.

The nanny fed indifferently, then stood sleepily in the first channeled light to chew her cud. I was observing her closely, sitting on a block of firewood outside my tent in the Swan Mountains. I judged her age to be three years. She had conceived during the rutting season of the previous fall. Now as she stood in the sun she made sudden hunching motions from time to time. I knew then that she had been

able to find enough food over winter to nourish both herself and the embryo growing within her. If my estimate of her age was correct, this would be her first pregnancy. What, I wondered, did she make of this heavy thing moving inside her?

The following day she fed little and slept in the shade of one of the Douglas firs. About six o'clock the next morning I found her standing near the same tree. Beside her, also standing—but quaking as it did—was a tiny goat, perhaps seven pounds in weight. Its coat was pale and wet, its eyes big and round, as though it were astounded by the size of the place—and the possibilities.

The mother licked her baby carefully. When she licked along its spine the infant straightened its legs and stood taller than before. Then it tottered beneath its mother, found one of her teats, and butted up against it to make the milk flow faster. Stimulation of the newborn animal in order to get it moving, standing, and finally nursing is one of the specific functions of licking. At the same time, the mother becomes imprinted with the smell of her offspring.

When it finished suckling, about three minutes after it started, the kid knelt —collapsed would be more accurate—and rested at its mother's feet.

Our view through the telescope was spellbinding. As we sat spooning cold meals past the tripod and into our mouths, the image unfolded and grew in miraculous patterns and with a speed that reminded me of movies in which time-lapse photography makes plants germinate, stretch upward, and flower in the space of one long breath.

Over half a century ago naturalist Ernest Thompson Seton reported seeing a mountain goat kid hopping into the air within ten minutes of its birth in captivity. A Montana old-timer I know tells a story of following a pregnant nanny for two days, intending to capture her kid and raise it himself. He swears he saw her give birth and reached the birthsite within half an hour, only to have the kid outhop him on the jumbled rocks. True or not, the tale is within the realm of possibility for this species. The kid I watched waited only slightly longer to begin hopping about.

Within five hours of being dropped onto the mountainside, it was ardently trying to climb it. Unable to walk very far without occasionally sprawling, the kid would skitter and wobble away from its mother and promptly place both forefeet up against whatever was higher than it was—ledges, boulders, tree trunks—and try to see what sort of progress it could make in a vertical direction. Then, returning home, it might try to climb the mound that was its bedded nanny.

Early that first day this prodigy gained the top of a medium-sized boulder. Without hesitation, as if its muscles had plans of their own, the baby sprang from there high into the air—only to land more on its nose than its feet. Then it went back up the boulder and repeated its performance, including the crash landing. In between nursing, resting, and attempting to go upward, the hours-old kid whirled in circles, made spasmodic hops, mewed and bleated in a voice that echoed through the valley, danced on its hind legs, and butted still non-existent horns at the sun bright sky. Its rubbery legs would not yet match all its inborn assurance. For her part, the nanny's attention to the tiny one was nearly absolute. Although she seemed restless and paced back and forth in the shade while her baby slept, the mother never went more than 20 feet from the infant. When the leaping baby lost its balance she was there below, so that it fell against her legs rather than toward the mountain's edge.

With her neck and head she gently nudged the baby uphill while it explored, and she made certain that during its many naps the youngster slept tucked against the summit side rather than the valley side of her thick coat. Even so, she was likely to awaken with the kid clambering atop her as it prepared to vault into space once again. Rising, stretching, and yawning, she would continue following its every move. I could hear her literally cry out when the baby took a hard spill, and she would rush over and lick and nuzzle it. The second day was warm and clear. Markedly faster on its feet after the first 24 hours, the baby was venturing farther, climbing more, and leaping higher. It was also falling harder, though not as often. Still, when it lifted a rear leg to scratch behind its ear, there was a fair amount of doubt as to whether the result would be a successfully scratched itch or yet another collision with the ground. No setback deterred the kid for long, though. In its hurry to live, the infant rarely walked anywhere. Instead, it bucked, scampered, and slid, then pawed at its mother's side if she was bedded, until she stood to let it refuel by nursing.

Douglas Chadwick

SKUNK CABBAGE

BOX ELDER

FERN

CORN LILY ▶

FUELED

Fueled
by a million
man-made
wings of fire—
the rocket tore a tunnel
through the sky—
and everybody cheered.
Fueled
only by a thought from God—
the seedling
urged its way
through the thicknesses of black—
and as it pierced
the heavy ceiling of the soil—
and launched itself
up into outer space—
no
one
even
clapped.

Marcie Hans

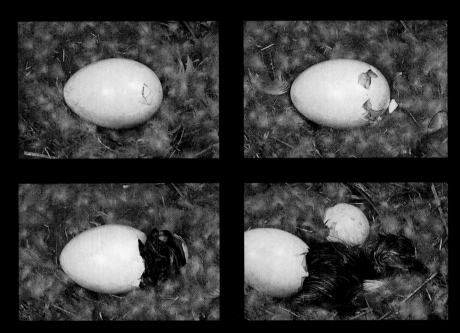

Facts are phantom; facts begin
With a bud, a seed, an egg.

A hero, a hoodlum, a little of both,
A toiling two-faced driven destiny,
Sleeps in the secret traceries of eggs.
If one egg could speak and answer the question,
    Egg, who are you, what are you, where did you
        come from and where are you going?

Let one egg tell and we would understand a billion eggs.

Carl Sandburg

PEEPING IN THE SHELL

On a Monday morning in May, I answered my phone and heard a joyful voice cry, "It's peeping in the shell! Isn't that wonderful!" I recognized George Archibald, the crane man. He was calling from Baraboo, Wisconsin, the headquarters of the International Crane Foundation, to tell me that a chick, still inside an egg laid 28 days before by a captive whooping crane, had survived a variety of hazards during incubation and was signalling its readiness to enter the world. "You've got to see it happen," he said. "Please get on a plane and come out." I told George I couldn't possibly go on such short notice. . . . But George's words echoed in my mind. Of course, I thought, it would be silly to drop everything and fly a thousand miles to see an egg hatch. What would there be to see? Just an egg—like the one I'd had for breakfast, only bigger. Hatching, I supposed, meant that the chick would simply break the shell and step out. Then I thought about whooping cranes: how marvellous it is that there are any at all; how marvellous that George Archibald and many other people are going to such extraordinary lengths to add to their number.

Surely this chick would have the strangest prenatal history of any ever hatched.

Its mother, Tex, was born at the San Antonio Zoo in 1967 and had been nursed through the first precarious weeks of her life by the zoo director, Fred Stark.

A weak chick, she would not have survived without his care, but an unfortunate side effect was that she had a lifelong preference for men over whooping cranes. This imprinting made her unrelentingly cold to normal mates. . . .

Tex later passed into the custody of George Archibald. Archibald knew that artificial insemination of Tex would present no problem. The problem was in Tex's head. A female bird ovulates in response to proper signals from her partner. In whooping cranes, these include close companionship and frequent interludes of courtship. George, who has both a flexible mind and a determined spirit, vowed he would bring Tex into breeding condition even if he had to do the courting himself.

When Tex arrived at Baraboo, George set up housekeeping with her. He put a cot in her quarters—a small frame building opening onto a grassy yard—and slept there for a month. . . . When spring came, George performed cranelike dances, leaping with out-

spread arms, bowing, and whirling. Tex joined in. To George's immense joy, she showed that she was ready for copulation. She was artificially inseminated, but. . . the egg was infertile. . . .

George danced with Tex for a second spring, and in 1978 she laid a fertile egg. "I heard the chick peeping, ready to hatch," George recalls, "and then it died. I was heartbroken."

. . .In 1979, George again courted Tex. . . . The egg was soft-shelled and broke. . . . Last spring, he decided to make another all-out effort. George and Tex staked out a nesting territory on a grassy hillside overlooking the crane pens. George

provided himself with a table, a typewriter, and a small shed, in which he could take shelter on wet days, and for six weeks he played the part of a loyal mate. When Tex rested beside him, George wrote letters. When she sought attention, he joined her in searching for food, gathering nesting material, and dancing. He sneaked away only after dark, and he returned at dawn. When Tex's readiness was apparent, she was artificially inseminated. At last, on May 3rd, when, by George's later admission, his nerves were reaching the breaking point, Tex laid the precious egg.

May 31st, 5:30 p.m. Seven hours after George's call, I have reached Baraboo. The egg rests on a bit of green carpet within an incubator that looks something like an old-fashioned wooden icebox except that it has two small, glass-paned windows on one side, giving a view of the interior. A fan hums as it circulates warm, humid air over the egg. Taking turns at the windows, we observe the egg: Archibald; Michael Putnam, a tall, dark-haired young man, who is the foundation's head aviculturist; and I.

Peering in, I see a brown-speckled greenish egg, about five inches long, cradled between two scraps of foam rubber. . . . Round end facing us, the egg rests mute, motionless, enigmatic. George points out a vital sign I've missed: a dime-size area of shell near the end shows a network of cracks, and at the center of the fracture there is a tiny puncture. . . . George is ebullient. Now, he explains, the chick should begin the pecking that will eventually liberate it. It should take no more than 36 hours. Longer than that means trouble.

"Let's see how he sounds," George suggests. Mike Putnam opens the incubator and makes a crooning sound. "Hello there! How're you doing?" A smile spreads over his face. "Good!" he exclaims . . . . George then offers me a turn. Sure enough, a tiny whispering sound emanates from the egg . . . .

7 p.m. The egg has remained motionless. George and I debate the value of an all-night vigil in order not to miss the magic moment when the chick steps out of the shell. Putnam is hungry and tired. Two young women who are assistants at the center volunteer to sit up with the egg and call us in the event of any change. We bid the egg good night.

June 1st, 9 a.m. I find George has been called away and Mike Putnam is in charge of the egg. It has made disappointingly little progress. A few more bits of shell have been chipped away creating a quarter-inch slot. Peering in I can detect something quivering inside.

10 a.m. No apparent change in the egg. I sit beside the incubator, occasionally glancing within. Sometimes I see movement inside the hole in the egg; mostly, the chick is quiet . . . .

10:30 a.m. Action! A fragment of shell has fallen from the rim of the hole in the egg. The tip of a beak sticks out, wavers, and falls back. I alert Mike. He goes over and peers in; then he opens the door. "Hi there!" he croons. A series of tiny, piping cries answers. The sound is eager and urgent but very, very small. "You're doing real good," Mike says encouragingly, and he shuts the door. The beak continues to nod and disappear, nod and disappear, as though the chick were desperately seeking contact.

"How much longer?" I ask.

"Lots longer," Mike replies. . . . At my request, Mike reviews the steps in hatching. They are more complicated and more perilous than I had imagined. . . . Hatching begins when the chick's hormones prompt it to start scratching. The scratching continues until the chick tears its natal sac and can thrust its beak into the air space between the sac and the shell. After the sac is torn, the lungs start to function. The chick is like a diver dependent on an air tank. It must reach the outer air, by pipping, before the oxygen in the air bubble is exhausted. Within 36 hours, it must peck a line of perforations circling the end of the egg. Then, ideally, the end of the shell will fall off, and set the chick free. To peck these perforations, the chick must rotate inside the egg. Mike calls it "spinning." It has been 20 hours since our chick pipped. It is time he started spinning.

Noon. The slot in the egg has lengthened. From time to time, a beak appears, waves back and forth, then sinks back, as though the chick were exhausted. Now and then, Mike opens the door and croons. Each time, the beak waves frantically, then disappears. I am beginning to feel anxious.

"Is the chick spinning yet?" I ask.

"Not yet," Mike says. "Give him time. It

takes an awful lot of energy to hatch."

2 p.m. Very little progress. . . . Mike opens the door and is greeted with frantic peeps—like cries for help. "Hi, kid!" he says softly. He picks up the egg and cradles it in his left hand. "Maybe this guy isn't going to spin. Maybe something is holding him up." With blunt scissors, Mike delicately nibbles at the edges of the aperture. The chick trills excitedly. Suddenly, I can see it: a rather awful shade of mauve, wet and leathery. I can see toes and beak and the quills of one wing all cramped together. Mike gently shoves the chick aside with the scissors. . . .

Why, I ask, doesn't he simply pull the chick out? Mike replies that timing is crucial. During the hours that the chick labors to perforate the shell, the blood vessels in the membrane that formerly supplied oxygen are drying up, and the yolk is being absorbed through the umbilical cord. If the chick were to be dragged from the shell before these steps were completed, it could bleed to death.

On the other hand, if it should fail to free itself at the right time it would also be in danger. In its cramped position, the lungs cannot fully expand; and this, combined with exhaustion, can asphyxiate it. Hearing this, I look at our poor egg and its valiantly struggling prisoner with reawakened anxiety. The chick seems infinitely frail, its task tremendous. . . .

5 p.m. The chick has worked the long claws of one foot against the edge of the egg and seems to be trying to push itself out. One wing is already clear. The long, frail neck lifts the head, then sinks to the green carpet in an exhausted coil. . . . Mike peers inside the shell. Looking over his shoulder, I can see glistening moisture and patches of blood. With a hypodermic, Mike dribbles in some drops of water and a styptic solution to prevent bleeding. He replaces the egg. Now the chick, looking exhausted, lies half in and half out. Mike reaches for a roll of white sticky tape and neatly fashions two shoulder straps, tethering the bird to what remains of the shell. "Too much blood and yolk," he explains. "I want to give him more time."

5:30 p.m. It has been a long day. I'm starved, but I don't want to miss anything. "Go ahead," Mike assures me. "This little guy isn't going anywhere right now."

6:30 p.m. I return to the incubator room. Mike is peering into the incubator, and he is smiling. "Look," he says. "He did it. He's O.K." There is the chick, lying on its breast, fully free at last. Its eyes are open, and its head nods in groggy triumph as it struggles to raise itself to its haunches. Its down is turning from mauve to reddish blond as it dries. "He just popped out," Mike says. "Doesn't he look great!" The chick raises its head and utters a tiny, piping whistle. It seems to say, "I am here. I am a whooping crane."

Faith McNulty

22

SERENDIPITY IN THE BRONX

On a warm, miserable morning last week I went up to the Bronx Zoo to see the moose calf and to break in a new pair of black shoes. I encountered better luck than I had bargained for. The cow moose and her young one were standing near the wall of the deer park below the monkey house, and in order to get a better view I strolled down to the lower end of the park, by the brook. The path there is not much traveled. As I approached the corner where the brook trickles under the wire fence, I noticed a red deer getting to her feet. Beside her, on legs that were just learning their business, was a spotted fawn, as small and perfect as a trinket seen through a reducing glass. They stood there, mother and child, under a gray beech whose trunk was engraved with dozens of hearts and initials. Stretched on the ground was another fawn, and I realized that the doe had just finished twinning. The second fawn was still wet, still unrisen. Here was a scene of rare sylvan splendor, in one of my five favorite boroughs, and I couldn't have asked for more. Even my new shoes seemed to be working out all right and weren't hurting much.

The doe was only a couple of feet from the wire, and I sat down on a rock at the edge of the footpath to see what sort of start young fawns get in the deep fastnesses of Mittel Bronx. The mother, mildly resentful of my presence and dazed from her labor, raised one forefoot and stamped primly. Then she lowered her head, picked up the afterbirth, and began dutifully to eat it, allowing it to swing crazily from her mouth, as though it were a bunch of withered beet greens. From the monkey house came the loud, insane hooting of some captious primate, filling the whole woodland with a loud hooroar. As I watched, the sun broke weakly through, brightened the rich red of the fawns, and kindled their white spots. Occasionally a sightseer would appear and wander aimlessly by, but of all who passed none was aware that anything extraordinary had occurred. "Looka the kangaroos!" a child cried. And he and his mother stared sullenly at the deer and then walked on.

In a few moments the second twin gathered all his legs and all his ingenuity and arose, to stand for the first time sniffing the mysteries of a park for captive deer. The doe, in recognition of his achievement, quit her other work and began to dry him, running her tongue against the grain and paying particular attention to the key points. Meanwhile the first fawn tiptoed toward the shallow brook, in little stops and goes, and started across. He

paused midstream to make a slight contribution, as a child does in bathing. Then, while his mother watched, he continued across, gained the other side, selected a hiding place, and lay down under a skunk-cabbage leaf next to the fence, in perfect concealment, his legs folded neatly under him. Without actually going out of sight, he had managed to disappear completely in the shifting light and shade. From somewhere a long way off a twelve-o'clock whistle sounded. I hung around awhile, but he never budged. Before I left, I crossed the brook myself, just outside the fence, knelt, reached through the wire, and tested the truth of what I had once heard: that you can scratch a new fawn between the ears without starting him. You can indeed.

E.B. White

MARMOTS

When Spring came
Leaves grew with a green fresh
feeling,
And the warmth of the sun
Was beginning to be felt,
And the Animals of the Earth
Awoke, breathing the fresh new
smell.
Of life all over again.

Tlingit Indian song

RED FOX

FLYCATCHERS

BLACK BEAR ▶

EVERYDAY MIRACLES

I have just learned to see praying mantis egg cases. Suddenly I see them everywhere; a tan oval of light catches my eye, or I notice a blob of thickness in a patch of slender weeds. As I write I can see the one I tied to the mock orange hedge outside my study window. It is over an inch long and shaped like a bell, or like the northern hemisphere of an egg cut through its equator. The full length of one of its long sides is affixed to a twig; the side that catches the light is perfectly flat. It has a dead straw, deadweed color, and a curious brittle texture, hard as varnish, but pitted minutely, like frozen foam. I carried it home this afternoon, holding it carefully by the twig, along with several others—they were as light as air. I dropped one without missing it until I got home and made a count.

Within the week I've seen 30 or so of these egg cases in a rose-grown field on Tinker Mountain, and another 30 in weeds along Carvin's Creek. One was on a twig of tiny dogwood on the mud lawn of a newly built house.

I think the mail-order houses sell them to gardeners at a dollar apiece.

It beats spraying, because each case contains between 125 to 350 eggs. If the eggs survive ants, woodpeckers, and mice—and most do—then you get the fun of seeing the new mantises hatch, and the smug feeling of knowing, all summer long, that they're out there in your garden devouring gruesome numbers of fellow insects all nice and organically.

* * *

I had once seen a mantis laying her eggs. It was several years ago that I witnessed this extraordinary procedure. . . .

She was upside-down, clinging to a horizontal stem of wild rose by her feet which pointed to heaven. Her head was deep in dried grass. Her abdomen was swollen like a smashed finger; it tapered to a fleshy tip out of which bubbled a wet, whipped froth. I couldn't believe my eyes. I lay on the hill this way and that, my knees in thorns and my cheeks in clay, trying to see as well as I could.

I poked near the female's head with a grass; she was clearly undisturbed, so I settled my nose an inch from that pulsing abdomen. It puffed like a concertina, it throbbed like a bellows; it roved, pumping, over the glistening, clabbered surface of the egg case testing and patting, thrusting and smoothing. It seemed to act so independently that I forgot the panting brown stick at the other end. The bubble creature seemed to have two eyes, a frantic little brain, and two busy, soft hands. It looked like a hideous, harried mother slicking up a fat daughter for a 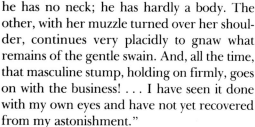 beauty pageant, touching her up, patting and hemming and brushing and stroking.

The male was nowhere in sight. The female had probably eaten him. Entomologist J. Henri Fabre says that, at least in captivity, the female will mate with and devour up to seven males, whether she has laid her egg cases or not.

The mating rites of mantises are well known: a chemical produced in the head of the male insect says, in effect, "No, don't go near her, you fool, she'll eat you alive." At the same time a chemical in his abdomen says, "Yes, by all means, now and forever yes."

While the male is making up what passes for his mind, the female tips the balance in her favor by eating his head. He mounts her. Fabre describes the mating, which sometimes lasts six hours, as follows: "The male, absorbed in the performance of his vital functions, holds the female in a tight embrace. But the wretch has no head; he has no neck; he has hardly a body. The other, with her muzzle turned over her shoulder, continues very placidly to gnaw what remains of the gentle swain. And, all the time, that masculine stump, holding on firmly, goes on with the business! . . . I have seen it done with my own eyes and have not yet recovered from my astonishment."

Annie Dillard

MUSHROOMS

Overnight, very
Whitely, discreetly,
Very quietly

Our toes, our noses
Take hold on the loam,
Acquire the air.

Nobody sees us
Stops us, betrays us;
The small grains make room.

Soft fists insist on
Heaving the needles,
The leafy bedding,

Even the paving,
Our hammers, our rams,
Earless and eyeless,

Perfectly voiceless,
Widen the crannies,
Shoulder through holes. We

Diet on water,
On crumbs of shadow,
Bland-mannered, asking

Little or nothing.
So many of us!
So many of us!

We are shelves, we are
Tables, we are meek,
We are edible,

Nudgers and shovers
In spite of ourselves.
Our kind multiplies:

We shall by morning
Inherit the earth.
Our foot's in the door.

Sylvia Plath

FROGS, FROGS, FROGS

One spring evening a couple of years ago, I was sitting in the brown leather chair in the living room reading the newspaper and minding my own business when I became aware that I was no longer alone. Looking up, I discovered that the three big windows that run from floor to ceiling were covered with frogs. There were hundreds of them, inch-long frogs with delicate webbed feet whose fingerlike toes  ended in round pads that enabled them to cling to the smooth surface of the glass.

From their toe structure, size and light-colored bellies, I supposed them to be spring peepers, *Hyla crucifer,* and went outside for a closer look. Sure enough, each pinkish-brownish frog had a back criss-crossed with the dark markings that give the species its scientific name.

I let my newspaper go and spent the evening watching them. These window climbers were silent; we usually are only aware of spring peepers at winter's end—I first hear their shrill bell-like mating calls in February from the pond up in the field. The males pro-duce the calls by closing their mouths and nasal openings and forcing air from their lungs over the vocal cords into their mouths, and then back over the vocal cords into the lungs again. This sound attracts the females to the pond, and when they enter the water the males embrace them, positioning their vents directly above those of the females. The females then lay their eggs, which the males fertilize with their milt. It is a 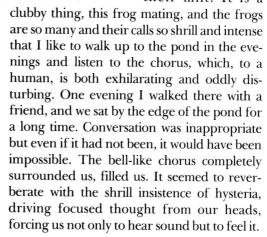 clubby thing, this frog mating, and the frogs are so many and their calls so shrill and intense that I like to walk up to the pond in the evenings and listen to the chorus, which, to a human, is both exhilarating and oddly disturbing. One evening I walked there with a friend, and we sat by the edge of the pond for a long time. Conversation was inappropriate but even if it had not been, it would have been impossible. The bell-like chorus completely surrounded us, filled us. It seemed to reverberate with the shrill insistence of hysteria, driving focused thought from our heads, forcing us not only to hear sound but to feel it.

Sue Hubbell

THE GREENING OF SUMMER

I count the spring year well begun when the aspen dangle their three-inch catkins, fuzzy earrings which dust the cabin deck with pollen. The catkins appear before the leaves do, open to the pollinating spring breezes. The amount of pollen is prodigious. When I cut a bouquet of spring branches, the table on which they sit is deep in pale sulphur-yellow pollen the next day.

Our log notes the appearance of the first leaves between May 14 and May 20, the third week in May consistent over the years. The leaves are a pale lucid green, circles cut out of green tissue paper and overlaid in shifting patterns. Now is the time to hang out the hammock and feel, in the chill warmth, intimations of summer. A week ago the light was too bright for reading comfortably in the grove; now the leaves make kaleidoscopic shadows on the book page.

The change between spring and summer in the aspen grove is not gradual. One day the wind is brisk and chill. The sun is warm on my back if I sit in a sheltered place, but the wind is sharp enough to mute the warmth and make my nose red. The ground is cold, still mostly brown with a few tiny sprouts of green seeking sun. The only plant in bloom around the cabin is a gray-green mound of golden smoke. A mourning-cloak butterfly tilts over my head and is gone, the first one of the year.

Then one day, not until the end of May, there is a perceptible change. There is scarcely more green on the ground, and the wind is just as capricious. But from the earth arises a warmth that envelops like a cocoon. The sun has finally heated the soil enough so that it is able to give back its radiation. The breeze is softer, more like cotton. The sun is warm on the back, now a reinforced warmth, not intermittent. The smell of pine rises from the ponderosa grove. Butterflies are more numerous, western painted lady and Butler's alpine and mountain blue. There is a humming and buzzing and clicking sewed together by the whirr of the hummingbird. He begins before the daisies are even open in the morning and is the last to settle in at night.

What there was the day before summer is still the same, still here, but there is just more of it, all molded together by the warmth that rises like a mist from the soil. Yesterday was spring, the chill spring of the mountains where night temperatures are still in the twenties and thirties, and the pump must be drained to prevent freezing. But one day it is all of a piece, and that day it is summer.

Ann Zwinger

REBIRTH OF A MOUNTAIN

September, 1985. The signs are small but startling: a smattering of rust-colored algae on rock, the pinpricks of animal tracks across a scorched landscape, a lone lupine blooming on a vast pumice plain like a rose on a businessman's gray suit. These are the delicate heralds of the healing of Mount St. Helens, five years after it exploded in the most destructive volcanic eruption in American history.

At 8:32 a.m. on May 18, 1980, an earthquake that measured 5.1 on the Richter scale triggered the largest landslide in recorded history and buried 24 square miles in 150 feet of rock, ash and mud. The top 1,313 feet of the 9,677-foot mountain were lopped off as easily as the crown of a boiled egg, instantly demoting Mount St. Helens from fifth to 77th on the list of Washington's tallest peaks.

A boiling plume of ash stretched 12 miles over the summit and, wafted by the winds, dusted roofs as far away as Minnesota and New Mexico. The death toll: 5,000 deer, 1,500 elk, 200 black bears, over a million birds, 11 million salmon and steelhead, and 57 people. Many scientists quickly pronounced the area a "dead zone" that would not revive for decades. They were wrong.

Scientists were surprised when burrowing insects and mammals, sheltered by snow and earth, appeared in supposedly sterile areas within weeks of the eruption. Fireweed, cattail and maple pushed resolutely through the ash, sprouting from roots the landslide had left miraculously intact.

As expected, life has also been imported from beyond the blast zone. Every summer day more than five tons of dead insects are blown mountainward from the surrounding forests, fertilizing the volcanic soil for new plant life. Seeds and spores are flown in by insects, birds and winds. Insects and vegetation have, in turn, lured back the mountain's traditional tenants, from bluebirds and hummingbirds to deer and elk.

The most spectacular rebirth is taking place within the volcano itself. The blast replaced the graceful conical peak with a jagged crater a mile wide and 2,000 feet deep. Subsequent volcanic activity has squeezed molten lava up into the crater like toothpaste from a tube. The lava hardened into a bump that, with successive eruptions, became a mound, then a hill, then a mountain within a mountain. If this growth continues, the dome will fill the crater and restore Mount St. Helens' original contours within 200 years.

Ed Barnes, Donna Haupt, George Howe Colt

AUTUMN RENEWAL

How pleasant to walk over beds of these fresh, crisp, and rustling fallen leaves...How beautiful they go to their graves! They that waved so loftily, how contentedly they return to dust again and are laid low, resigned to lie and decay at the foot of the tree and afford nourishment to new generations of their kind. How they are mixed up, all species—oak and maple and chestnut and birch! They are about to add a leaf's breadth to the depth of the soil. We are all the richer for their decay. Nature is not cluttered with them. She is a perfect husbandman; she stores them all.

Henry David Thoreau

MARCH 9

I think of spring as a beginning only because the human mind and habit tend that way. Human creatures like to count. They like matters to be neatly parceled, with beginnings and endings. That is one reason we devised the calendar and invented the clock, and one reason we call sundown the end of the day and sunrise the beginning. But few matters have such neat beginnings and endings. There is a continuance, a progression, or at least a continuity. Spring is a quickening, but it is no more a beginning than is high noon or mid-July. It is only another aspect of that which is continuous.

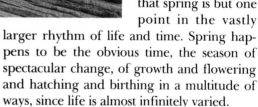

There are, to be sure, annual plants and seasonal insects as well as those that live on from year to year. But annual plants grow from seeds, and the insects come from some egg form. The seeds and the eggs are no more than capsulated life carried over from one generation to the next. Somewhere along the path of evolution those plants and those insects found it would be more advantageous to entrust their precious germ of life to an egg or a dormant seed than to try to hoard it in a root or a body over the winter.

There are also such plants as the bristlecone pines of California that have lived as growing trees for at least 4,600 years. And there are periodic locusts that live in the ground as grubs fifteen years or more before they emerge, acquire wings, eat, mate, create a din, lay eggs, and die, all within an adult life of only a few weeks. They merely prove that spring is but one point in the vastly larger rhythm of life and time. Spring happens to be the obvious time, the season of spectacular change, of growth and flowering and hatching and birthing in a multitude of ways, since life is almost infinitely varied.

We see life burgeoning. We are made aware of life and sometimes we celebrate its existence. More often we merely celebrate our own existence and indulge our pride in being what we call a superior form of life.

Hal Borland

CREDITS

PHOTO CREDITS

Cover: Frans Lanting. **1, 2:** Steven C. Wilson/Entheos. **4-5:** Bob McKeever/Tom Stack and Associates **6:** Stephen J. Krasemann/DRK Photo. **9:** Frans Lanting. **10-11:** Stan Osolinski. **13:** Tom and Pat Leeson. **14: top and middle,** David Cavagnaro; **bottom,** Art Wolfe. **14-15:** David Cavagnaro; **16:** all by Breck P. Kent; **16-17:** Charles Krebs. **18-19:** Jeff Foott. **20:** William C. Gause. **23:** Frank Oberle. **24:** Leonard Lee Rue III/Bruce Coleman Inc. **26:** Wolfgang Bayer. **27:** both by Charles Krebs. **28: left,** Breck P. Kent; **right,** Art Wolfe. **29:** Thomas Kitchin/Tom Stack and Associates **30:** Patti Murray/Animals Animals. **31:** F.E. Unverhau/Animals Animals. **32:** Kerry Givens. **34:** John Gerlach/DRK Photo. **35:** Zig Leszczynski/Animals Animals. **36:** David Cavagnaro. **38-39:** Robert Comport/Earth Scenes. **40:** Gary Braash. **42-43:** Charles Krebs. **44:** David Muench. **45:** David Muench.

TEXT CREDITS

We thank these publishers, authors, or their representatives for permission to reprint their material.

Song to Pull Down the Clouds (p. 5), from *American Indian Prose and Poetry*, Margot Astrov, ed. Peter Smith Publishers.

A Sense of Wonder (p. 7), excerpts from *The Sense of Wonder*, by Rachel Carson. Copyright © 1956 by Rachel L. Carson. Copyright renewed 1984 by Roger Christie. Reprinted by permission of Harper & Row, Publishers, Inc.

Return of the Geese (p. 8), from *A Sand County Almanac and Sketches Here and There* by Aldo Leopold. Copyright © 1949, 1977 by Oxford University Press, Inc. Reprinted by permission.

Mountain Birth (pp. 10-13), condensed from *A Beast the Color of Winter*, by Douglas H. Chadwick. Copyright © 1983 by Douglas H. Chadwick. Reprinted with permission of Sierra Club Books.

ABOUT THE COVER

The eggs on the cover represent only a fraction of the collection of about 800,000 eggs housed at a Los Angeles museum, the Western Foundation of Vertebrate Zoology. The museum's curator, Ed Harrison, has spent more than 30 years rounding up this natural history treasure, which includes about 250 individual collections from all over the world. Gathered mostly between the mid-1800s and World War II, these eggs provide a resource for scientists studying endangered birds and other species. Since 1968, scientists have used the eggs in more than 2,000 studies.

Photo by Frans Lanting

Library of Congress Cataloging-in-Publication Data

Beginnings.

   (Gifts of nature)
   1. Nature.   I. National Wildlife Federation.   II. Series.
QH1.B414   1989   508
89-8276
ISBN 0-945051-10-7

STAFF FOR THIS BOOK

Howard Robinson, *Editorial Director*

Elaine S. Furlow, *Senior Editor*

Donna Miller, *Design Director*

Debby Anker, *Illustrations Editor*

Ellen Cohen, *Designer*

Michele Morris, *Research Editor*

Cei Richardson, *Editorial Assistant*

Vi Kirksey, *Editorial Secretary*

Paul Wirth, *Quality Control*

Margaret E. Wolf, *Permissions Editor*

NATIONAL WILDLIFE FEDERATION
1400 Sixteenth St., N.W., Washington, D.C. 20036-2266

NATIONAL WILDLIFE FEDERATION

Jay D. Hair, *President and Chief Executive Officer*

William W. Howard Jr., *Executive Vice President and Chief Operating Officer*

Alric H. Clay, *Senior Vice President, Administration*

Francis A. DiCicco, *Vice President, Financial Affairs and Treasurer*

Lynn A. Greenwalt, *Vice President and Special Assistant to the President for International Affairs*

John W. Jensen, *Vice President, Development*

S. Douglas Miller, *Vice President, Research and Education*

Kenneth S. Modzelewski, *Vice President, Promotional Activities*

Sharon L. Newsome, *Acting Vice President, Resources Conservation*

Larry J. Schweiger, *Vice President, Affiliate and Regional Programs*

Stephanie C. Sklar, *Vice President, Public Affairs*

Robert D. Strohm, *Vice President, Publications*

Joel T. Thomas, *General Counsel and Secretary*